SKETCHES OF

MANCHURIAN BATTLE-FIELDS

SKETCHES OF MANCHURIAN BATTLE-FIELDS

WITH A VERBAL DESCRIPTION OF SOUTHERN MANCHURIA

AN AID TO THE STUDY OF THE RUSSO-JAPANESE WAR

BY

MAJOR A. I. R. GLASFURD, P.S.C.
INDIAN ARMY

The Naval & Military Press Ltd

Reproduced by kind permission of the Central Library,
Royal Military Academy, Sandhurst

Published by
The Naval & Military Press Ltd
Unit 10, Ridgewood Industrial Park,
Uckfield, East Sussex,
TN22 5QE England
Tel: +44 (0) 1825 749494
Fax: +44 (0) 1825 765701
www.naval-military-press.com
www.military-genealogy.com
© The Naval & Military Press Ltd 2010

The Naval & Military Press ...

...offer specialist books for the serious student of conflict. The range of titles stocked covers the whole spectrum of military history with titles on uniforms, battles, official histories, specialist works containing Medal Rolls and Casualties Lists, and numismatic titles for medal collectors and researchers.

The innovative approach they have to military bookselling and their commitment to publishing have made them Britain's leading independent military bookseller.

In reprinting in facsimile from the original, any imperfections are inevitably reproduced and the quality may fall short of modern type and cartographic standards.

INTRODUCTION

MAJOR GLASFURD was one of a party of officers who was sent on an official visit from the Staff College in India to the battle-fields of Manchuria, in 1907.

I accompanied this party, and saw Major Glasfurd execute the sketches which are now reproduced in this volume. I consider the sketches are true and accurate representations of ground itself not at all easy to portray.

The sketches must not be considered only for their artistic merit, but also, and chiefly, for their military value.

They will enable the student of the Manchurian War, who cannot himself visit the scene of the fighting, to take in the character and military features of the country.

If the student will identify on the map the point from which each sketch was taken, and adjust the sketch with reference to it, he will be rewarded by a really clear view of the country.

It is necessary to remark that these sketches were made in the month of May, a time when crops have not attained any height. When the *kao-liang* rises, as it does later in the year, many of the smaller features and details of the ground are, I understand, completely hidden. This must be borne in mind in comparing the accounts of the battles with the pictures in this volume.

T. CAPPER,
BRIGADIER-GENERAL,
Commandant, Staff College, Quetta, India.

June 29, 1909.

PREFACE

These drawings, and the verbal description which accompanies them, are published as an aid to the study of the Russo-Japanese War of 1904-1905. It is hoped they will be found useful by students of that campaign, whichever of its numerous histories they may be reading.

The sketches and notes were made in May, 1907, when, with the exception of the country north of the Mukden area, all of the Manchurian battle-fields were visited and studied in detail. It was possible, therefore, to select the various panoramas with care as to their military value, and to draw them from what, after deliberation, appeared to be the most suitable points of view.

The drawings are to scale—that is to say, they were, for the sake of accuracy, constructed on a system of horizontal and vertical measurements, and fractions thereof. In some cases the original scale of "handspreads" has been preserved, and is shown at the top of the sketch; in others the pencil-marks used in construction have, unfortunately, been rubbed out. The "handspread" referred to is the distance between the tips of thumb and fourth finger of the observer, when those fingers are fully separated and extended at arm's length. In most individuals this measurement will be found to produce an angle of about 20 degrees.

Some of the reproductions have been slightly reduced from his originals, and lithographically copied, by the author himself; the others have been copied from the originals by another draughtsman, most of them extremely well.

In order to make the location of the sketches quite clear for the reader, rough maps have been included; and on these the angle comprised by the extent of view of each sketch is shown by a shaded sector, numbered to correspond with the sketch. This will also remove any doubt arising from the frequent divergences in spelling of Manchurian place-names, whether their orthography be after the Chinese, Japanese, or European style. For instance, TEH-LITZ (Chinese) and TOKORIJEN (Japanese) are the same as TELISSU, or, as the Russians call it, WAFANGO.

Heights are shown, in feet, thus: $+350'$; and, except when otherwise stated, denote heights above sea-level.

Ranges, in yards, from viewpoint of sketch, thus: 1200^x.

In order to facilitate the arrangement of the verbal description, the various battle-fields have been grouped, according to the type of country to which they belong (*vide* Index).

The study of a campaign, and its maps, is, of course, best aided by a visit to the ground itself; but for those who are unable to do this the landscape sketch is the next best appeal to the eye, and is, moreover, superior to a photograph in depicting military features of ground.

Since the delineator of these sketches was only able to begin his drawings in MANCHURIA after the lectures, discussions, and notes on the battle-fields had been concluded, and as a tardy return to quarters inevitably resulted in the discovery that all available food had long since disappeared under the attack of his twenty-nine healthy fellow-workers, it cannot truthfully be said that the conception of this small volume was entirely devoid of pain. But this will have its compensation if a useful idea has been given of the theatre of war—past or future—in Southern Manchuria.

A. I. R. G.

NOTE

In order to obtain the best panoramic effect from these sketches, they should be held close to the eyes, at a distance of not more than six to seven inches from them.

When held thus, the head of the reader will have to be turned right and left in order to observe the whole of the panorama depicted—just as would be the case were he looking at the country itself.

INDEX TO LETTERPRESS

(Battle-fields being grouped according to type of country)

	PAGES
I. KWANTUNG PENINSULA, AND GENERAL NOTES	1—6

    INCLUDING THE BATTLE-FIELDS OF—
        PORT ARTHUR.
        NANSHAN.

	PAGES
II. THE LIAO PLAINS AND FOOTHILLS	7—9

    INCLUDING THE BATTLE-FIELDS OF—
        LIAOYANG, with
            SHOUSHANPU
            MANJUYAMA
        SHAHO, with
            YENTAI COUNTRY
            PUTILOFF HILL
        MUKDEN (EXCEPTING THE FAR EAST)

	PAGES
III. THE HIGHER HILLY REGIONS	10—13

    INCLUDING—
        TELISSU
        ANPING
        KOSAREI, OR HUNG-SHA-LING
        HILLS S.-E. OF LIAOYANG
        TALING
        PENHSIHU AND TAITSE VALLEY
        CHAOTAO
        MOTIENLING
        KUROKI'S LINE OF COMMUNICATIONS

	PAGES
IV. THE YALU	14—15

    INCLUDING—
        YALU
        HAMATUN

INDEX TO SKETCHES AND MAPS

MAP	SKETCH		
A	A.	Port Arthur:	Eastern Defences.
	B.	„ „	Northern Defences.
	C.	„ „	View N.-W. from Wangtai.
	D.	„ „	Two Comparative Views of Harbour
	E.	„ „	203-Metre Hill from S.-W.
	F.	„ „	203-Metre Hill from N.
B	G.	Nanshan.	
C	H.	Telissu: View from E.	
	J.	Telissu: View from W.	
D	K.	Shoushanpu.	
	L.	Russian Positions S.-E. of Liaoyang.	
	M.	Kuroki's Crossing of the Taitse-ho	
	N.	Manjuyama.	
	O.	Kosarei, or Hung-sha-ling	
	P.	Kung-chang-ling	
	Q.	Chaotao.	
E	R.	Putiloff Hill.	
	S.	Terayama and San-kwai-seki-san.	
	T.	Taling.	
D	U.	Kanin's Action near Penhsihu.	
F	V.	Motienling from E.	
	W.	Motienling from W.	
G	X.	Yalu from Japanese Side.	
	Y.	Yalu from Russian Side.	
	Z.	Hamatun.	

JAPANESE WAR MEMORIAL AT MUKDEN: A COLOSSAL RIFLE-CARTRIDGE.

To face p. 1.

DESCRIPTION OF MANCHURIA

I

KWANTUNG PENINSULA, AND GENERAL NOTES

Preliminary note. For facility of description, the various battlefields and parts of the theatre of war in MANCHURIA have been grouped according to the type of country to which they belong (*vide* Index).

Where they differ from the general type described a separate note has been inserted.

Much of the general description of the KWANTUNG PENINSULA will be found to apply to the rest of MANCHURIA, and subsequent descriptions will, therefore, be confined to a notice of any divergences from it.

Kwantung Peninsula: General character (*Vide* Sketches A to G). The KWANTUNG PENINSULA is more or less hilly throughout, the hills rising rather abruptly from the low ground. The larger valleys that intersect them are shallow, and wind their way gently towards the low, muddy shores of the surrounding sea.

Hills and valleys: Height and character. The higher hills average about 1,000 feet above sea-level, rising in places to about 1,500 feet or more. They consist of a rather confused tangle of irregular heights, with spurs thrown off in every direction. This gives its indented character to the coast-line. The watershed follows approximately the centre of the peninsula.

PORT ARTHUR

The higher hills continue from the neighbourhood of DALNY to a point about five miles N.-E. of PORT ARTHUR. At this point the range—

here named the WOLF HILLS, and along which ran the JAPANESE investing line—is interrupted by broad, open valleys that cross the peninsula from the neighbourhood of LOUISA BAY to TAKI BAY. S.-W. of these lies the amphitheatre of low hills, averaging about 500 feet above sea-level, which surround the basin of PORT ARTHUR itself, and on which its defences of the fortress were constructed. Yet farther to the S.-W. the main range again rises, and terminates, at the extremity of the peninsula, in the lofty mass of the LAO-TI-SHAN.

More detailed character of hills. The summits of most of the loftier hills are rocky and broken, but their slopes, and practically all the lower hills, are covered with a loose, friable, and rather sandy soil, overlying a disintegrated and rubbly subsoil.

This gives the hillsides a smooth and rounded contour, more convex than concave.

Surface soil. The surface soil is particularly easy to excavate, except in a few places on hill slopes and ridges, where it may be rocky.

The result of the excavations and levellings for the construction of the PORT ARTHUR forts and defences, and their subsequent destruction by shell-fire, mine and spade, has, therefore, been to turn the hilltops on which they stood into vast rubbish-heaps of stony débris.

Vegetation. The hillsides are bare and devoid of vegetation, except for a very short and mossy covering of thin grass. During the severe winter, and for some time after it, this grass is withered to a curious dull olive-grey tint. There are a few insignificant patches of very low, thin, pinous scrub in sheltered parts of the hills.

Colour of soil and surface, affecting question of invisibility. The light reddish-yellow colour of the soil and the smooth grassy surface of all the higher ground combine to make the slightest scratch on the surface of these hills stand most sharply out, thus rendering it practically impossible to conceal trenches and excavations. Indeed, on these hills it would seldom be possible to conceal troops in action, even if widely extended. "Invisibility," therefore, except in the case of old-established field-works, is practically out of the question. The sharp divergence in colour between the soil and its natural covering also causes a most distinct line of demarcation between the green-grey hills and the red plough-land.

The valleys at first sight appear to be of quite open character, with gentle undulations; but closer inspection shows that the deep, soft, reddish soil is seamed with very numerous sharply-cut ravines and watercourses (very similar to the "nullahs" of India), which ramify in every direction—from broad main channels or miniature valleys, with level bottoms, to minor clefts and hollows. These watercourses, many of them from 30 to 50 feet deep, push far into the surrounding hills, in the sides of which they have cut deep gashes, and afford an extraordinary amount of cover for troops. Numerous field-banks, terraces, dips and folds also accident the ground, and roads or tracks are in many cases "hollow."

The valleys: Detailed character.

"Cover" afforded by ground.

Except for these impediments, troops of all arms can move along the valleys and on the gentler slopes of the hills. Infantry can go practically anywhere. There are no fences, nor are the fields enclosed in any way. The soft plough is tenacious and difficult to cross when wet.

The valleys and lower hill-slopes are much cultivated, the staple crops being beans and millet. From about October to June bare plough and furrow prevail. During the remainder of the year crops—mainly *kao-liang*, or giant millet—cover the ground.

Crops.

Kao-liang is practically identical with *jowari*, or *jowar*, of India, and, since when fully grown it attains an average height of 8 to 10 feet, it naturally affords complete cover from view for troops of all arms. The Japanese, however, experienced difficulty in maintaining their direction when moving through it. *Kao-liang* is at its height from early August until the harvest. It is cut exactly like *jowari* (with a slanting upward slice of the sickle), and its sharp-pointed, firmly-rooted stumps offer a similar obstacle after it has been reaped.

Villages.
The Chinese villages that dot the plain and valleys, at intervals of a mile or so, to a certain extent resemble those of India, although they are rather of the prosperous farmsteading type, and built in more straggling fashion. In the KWANTUNG PENINSULA they are mostly built of mud and stone, with thatched or tiled roofs, and are enclosed by loose stone dykes. The walls are thick; but where entirely mud-built do not offer a complete obstacle to rifle bullets, except when frozen hard in the winter. The houses are more commodious and offer better shelter and quarters for troops than is the rule in India. A few scattered poplar and pear trees grow about the villages, but the rest of the country is quite devoid of wood.

Roads and tracks.
The villages are connected by rough, straggling, country tracks, difficult to traverse after rain. There are no regular roads except those constructed by the Russians in the vicinity of PORT ARTHUR and its defences, and, of course, at DALNY.

Railways (*Vide* General Map).
The Russian gauge was originally 5 feet. This was subsequently altered by the Japanese, by shifting a rail, to their standard gauge of 3 feet 6 inches.

Rivers.
The small streams draining the peninsula flow in very shallow sandy beds after they gain the wider portions of the valleys. Except in the rainy season, they contain a mere trickle of water. Their higher and steeper-banked courses are usually quite dry. Near the low-lying coast and little estuaries their banks are muddy, sandy, and in places slightly marshy.

Water is fairly plentiful and good, and there are few or none of the water difficulties that exist in equally arid-looking parts of India. Water is obtained from wells and from the larger streams.

HOUSE IN SUI-SHI-YING VILLAGE, WHERE NOGI AND STOESSEL MET TO ARRANGE TERMS FOR THE CAPITULATION OF PORT ARTHUR.

To face p. 4.

MANCHURIAN HILL COUNTRY

LOW HILLS: SUMMIT OF 203-METRE HILL.

HIGH HILLS: SUMMIT OF KOSAREI.

The sketches represent the LIAOTUNG country as it is in spring—late April and early May, that is to say—and about six weeks to two months after the break-up of the severe Manchurian winter.

Climate and seasons.

At this season of spring the ground has been prepared for crops, most of which have already been sown. The weather is still cold and bleak, especially while the icy Mongolian wind is blowing. Some scanty green grass is beginning to sprout on the hills and fallow ground. Rain falls, off and on, at this season, but the really wet weather is not ushered in till late in June. The sun is sometimes very hot in the summer, and exhausting for troops whose clothing is unsuitable.

Fairer weather sets in about September, and the crops are cut and off the ground by October.

From November onwards the rigorous Manchurian winter sets in, the ground itself being frozen to a depth of about 3 feet. This icy grasp is not relaxed until the following month of March, and is most severe in late January and early February. Snow falls during the winter, but in no large amount; it seldom lies, except in small patches, and there thinly.

The military operations round PORT ARTHUR were prosecuted through all these varying seasons, and this must not be lost sight of in studying the history of the siege.

Finally, it should be borne in mind that, like most countries where the seasons are sharply separated and marked by large variations of temperature, MANCHURIA is unlike WESTERN EUROPE.

Recapitulation.

Where plain or valley meets or alternates with hilly ground, as in KWANTUNG, the country is rather like that in the Punjab about Attock and Rawalpindi, but without the system of extraordinary "nullahs" common to that country. The lower hills of MANCHURIA are of a smoother, rolling character, and its few mountains rise into serrated rocky ridges.

NANSHAN

The country here is typically KWANTUNG in character. The central range or backbone of higher hills is, however, interrupted at the ISTHMUS OF KINCHAU. This isthmus is quite low-lying. It is overlooked from the N.-E. and N. by the lofty masses of MOUNT SAMPSON and contiguous ranges; and from the S.-W. by the heights near NANKWANLING.

Vide Sketch G.

The block of low hills—hillocks, rather—which occupies the centre of the isthmus, and on which the Russians took up their defensive position, is of the same character as similar features near PORT ARTHUR, already described. It rises to a maximum height of about 350 feet above the low country, and is deeply penetrated by very sharp-cut "nullahs," especially on the S.-W. side. The soil is, for the most part, quite soft and easy to excavate; but concealment of earthworks is, if possible, even more out of the question than about PORT ARTHUR. At the time of the fight the surrounding country was as shown in the sketches—bare, open plough, but considerably accidented, and affording a fair amount of cover for Infantry lying down during its advance to the attack.

Slopes more convex than concave.

The foreshore of the shallow inlets of KINCHAU and HAND BAYS is flat and muddy.

The isthmus, except on the NANSHAN ridges, which are rather difficult for wheels, can be traversed freely by troops of all arms.

II

THE LIAO PLAINS AND FOOTHILLS

The great battles of Liaoyang, the Shaho, and, to a lesser extent, Mukden, were fought in this region, where the wide Liao Plain meets the outlying foothills of the main range.

Vide Sketches K, M, N, R, S.

The main hilly mass sends out numbers of gradually diminishing ranges and spurs, which merge gently into the plain, sometimes pushing a long ridge into the flat country, as at Shoushanpu; at other points breaking up into minor isolated hills and knolls, as about Yentai.

These lower foothills are of the same type as in Kwantung—perhaps a trifle rockier; but are not so full of deep "nullahs."

The Liao Plains are very like the great plains of Northern India, but are not wooded to quite such an extent. They are highly cultivated, level, and monotonous, with some gentle undulations. At rare intervals there may be a very slight knoll. About Mukden, however, the plains are much more rolling in character, and rather more wooded.

The soil of the Liao Plains, when wet, is not quite so tenacious as that of the cultivated plains of India, as it contains a greater proportion of sand. It seems, however, to have proved a great obstacle to movement in wet weather, when it is said to have rendered the cavalry of both sides almost immobile.

Soil.

The soil is brown in colour, redder near high ground. There are no fences or field-boundaries to hamper movement. Chinese graveyards are scattered about at intervals of half a mile or so, and are quite small unfenced oases of grass and bushes, with sometimes a little grove of trees, usually stunted firs. Most of these trees, however, were cut down during the war.

The regular ridges, ploughed by the careful Chinese cultivator, make the "going" rather difficult and exhausting, especially, it is said, in winter, when the interminable furrows are frozen hard.

Movement generally, however, is freer in MANCHURIA during winter. There is practically no snow, the ground is hard, with a dry and friable surface, and the frozen rivers can be crossed anywhere, if the steepness of their banks does not interfere.

Movement.

The villages are as in KWANTUNG, perhaps a trifle larger, but here they are almost entirely built of mud, or of mud mixed with *kao-liang* stalks. Courtyard walls vary from 4 to 8 feet in height, and about 18 inches to 2 feet thick. Villages are connected by country tracks. Villages afford cover from view, and a certain amount of cover from fire, especially when walls are frozen.

Villages.

They also afford that shelter from the severe winter weather which is absolutely indispensable for human beings.

The large "first to fourth class" towns, such as LIAOYANG, MUKDEN, FUSHUN, etc., are typical North Chinese walled towns, with, if on the railway-line, Russian military cantonments grouped about the railway-stations.

Large towns.

Even the "Mandarin" roads are worse than most Indian *kutcha* roads, and are unbridged and utterly uncared for.

Roads.

Water is plentiful from rivers, ponds, streams, and wells. The latter do not freeze in the severest winter.

The smaller rivers or streams are extremely shallow, flowing in broad sandy beds, only a few feet below the level of the surrounding country.

Rivers.

The TAITSE-HO and the HUN-HO are, however, typical large Manchurian rivers. Their average breadth is 250 yards, average depth 3 feet; current varies from 2 to 5 miles per hour. In the hilly

ANTUNG-MUKDEN LIGHT RAILWAY.

To face p. 9.

country their beds are shingly; in the plains they are composed of mud and sand.

The SHAHO is a minor river, with moderate banks, and shingly and sandy bed, rather like the large perennial Indian "nullahs"; and the SHI-LI-HO is merely a large ditch, very deep-cut, its centre occupied by an insignificant, sluggish stream, a few feet wide, flowing in a muddy bottom. Its presence is not to be divined at a few hundred yards' distance.

These smaller rivers do not appear to be troubled much by floods. Nearly all the rivers are bordered by straggling patches of willow-scrub.

Crops are almost entirely *kao-liang*, a sea of which covers the country towards autumn. There is little cover from fire, except in villages.

About MUKDEN, especially in the country to the S.-W. of it and down the HUN-HO, the country is more enclosed by patches of willow-scrub and the small fir and oak woods that cover some of the Chinese graveyards; W. and N. of MUKDEN are a few patches, that to the WEST being of large extent, of dense pine and oak woods, surrounding the Imperial MANCHU tombs.

Vegetation.

The seasons and climate of the LIAO PLAINS are as in KWANTUNG. Terrible dust-storms occur during winter, blown up by fierce icy winds, and obscuring vision beyond about 200 yards.

The light railway from MUKDEN to ANTUNG, on the YALU, is of 2 feet 6 inch gauge. It was not quite completed at the time of the campaign in that part of the country.

III

THE HIGHER HILLY REGIONS

GENERALLY speaking, this region cannot be termed mountainous. It is difficult to understand how so misleading a term came to be applied to the country through which KUROKI'S Army—and, to a lesser degree, that of NODZU—made its way towards LIAOYANG.

Vide Sketches H, J, L, O, P, Q, T, U, V, W.

In reality it is a country of steep and extremely confused hills, mostly rather bare, and possesses only a few higher ridges that could possibly be called mountains.

Perhaps the awe-inspiring names given to portions of the range by the Chinese, such as " Great Pass " and " Heaven-Scratching Pass," have something to do with some of the highly-coloured and exaggerated descriptions which have been given.

The surface and contour of these hills are mostly of the KWANTUNG type, and the main differences lie in the vegetation.

Telissu, Anping, Kosarei (or Hungshaling), and Taling (*vide* Sketches L, P, T, H, J).

In their westward portions, where they approach the LIAO PLAINS, the hills are of the barer description, although more wooded than in KWANTUNG, with copses on their flanks, and willow and poplar patches in the valleys.

As the central part of the hilly tract is reached, vegetation increases; but it is only small stunted oak, elm, and a little fir. Southward of the MOTIENLING, and in the country N. of FENGHWANGCHENG, the troubled sea of very confused little hills is covered with a dense clothing of dwarf elm and oak coppice. Here also the soil is shingly in character, and much looser.

Penhsihu (*vide* Sketch U).

DESCRIPTION OF MANCHURIA

Motienling (*vide* Sketches V, W.)

About FENGHWANGCHENG the hills once more become barer and lower, with the exception of the PHŒNIX MOUNTAIN, which is a lofty serrated chain of barren rock pinnacles.

Kuroki's Line of Communication.

A remarkable feature of the Manchurian ranges is the system of valleys—very different valleys to those of the Indian Frontier. The country, indeed, would be better described as smooth, open, level valleys, separated by "lumpy" hills, than as hilly country with easy, long valleys.

The valleys are almost all long, level, and broad—about 1,000 yards wide on the average—linked up with each other by usually very easy passes, and, except when flooded, traversable without trouble by all arms.

Few of the "passes" would be recognizable by us in India as such. The TALING (or "Great Pass"), N.-W. of PENHSIHU, is a ridiculous little

Vide Sketch T.

col connecting some low hills at the head of a typically easy valley, with GUNKIYAMA, a retiring little knoll—about which, by the way, a very mountainous epic has been woven—lying still lower.

Vide Sketch W.

The MOTIENLING, or "Heaven-Scratching Pass," itself is rather like the lower wooded hills at the foot of the WESTERN GHAUTS, near BOMBAY, or those about Windermere in the English Lake District.

Almost the only obstacle to movement in the valleys is that caused by the continually repeated crossing of the winding rivers, which, though ordinarily shallow in their pebbly beds, are liable to flood during heavy rain. It was this that so greatly disorganized KUROKI's lines of communication in July, 1904.

The CHAOTAO VALLEY and neighbourhood are to some extent like

Vide Sketch Q.

TELISSU (*q.v.*), though rather barer, and are remarkable for a rocky and precipitous bluff that closely follows the right bank of the SHIHO RIVER.

TELISSU

The country in which this battle took place is perhaps slightly different to what has hitherto been described.

It differs chiefly from the typical KWANTUNG country in respect of the wide, shallow valley of the FOOCHOW (or FU-CHIAO) RIVER, and the vegetation. At the time of the battle the country was much as it is shown in the landscape sketches.

Vide **Sketches H and J.**

The FOOCHOW river-bed, here traversing a very hilly district, averages about a mile in width; and, except during heavy rain, contains little more than a shallow thread of water winding through a broad sandy bed, which latter in its turn traverses a level expanse of alluvial cultivated soil.

This part of the country does not seem to be liable to heavy floods, a rise in the waters of the FOOCHOW RIVER here apparently spreading over the level sand, without any great deepening or acceleration of the main current.

The valley and its tributary ravines are rather thickly studded with willow and poplar trees, which are usually disposed in rows and clumps, the latter sometimes forming considerable open woods.

Copses of low oak, wild cherry, and plum, with other small trees and scrub, cling to the hillsides here and there; with, more rarely, little spinneys of stunted fir-trees.

The valley is bordered on each side by low and bare rolling hills, which spring abruptly to a maximum height of about 400 feet above the river, and are intersected by rather deep watercourses.

Farther back from this border of lower hills (except for that portion between TELISSU RAILWAY-STATION and TAFANGSHIN, where there are no high hills), the ground rises rather steeply to the higher hills, which have a maximum height of from 1,200 to 1,500 feet above the valley. The higher tops, such as LUNGTANSHAN, which lies closely to the N.-N.-W. of the RAILWAY-STATION, are very rocky and precipitous. RINKIATUN, CHIANGTZUSHAN, and the mass of heights lying E. of the FOOCHOW RIVER, are of a similar nature; the last-named being strewn with boulders, with stone-shoots down its sides.

Small Chinese villages or farm-steadings, enclosed by stone dykes, dot the FOOCHOW VALLEY, and are also found nestling in groves of willow, poplar, and pear trees up its sheltered winding branches. Cultivation is mainly restricted to the more level country, though there are some terraced fields where the hillside soil is deep. There is more grass in this country than in KWANTUNG, and in rainy weather the aspect of the hills is not altogether unlike the more elevated portions of the English Lake District.

Other points as already noted.

IV

THE YALU AND HAMAT'UN

This country possesses a character of its own.

Vide Sketches X, Y, Z.
The high, rocky, and serrated spur (named Teng-Shi-Shan), thrown off from the Phœnix Mountain of Fenghwangcheng, ceases abruptly about nine miles N. of Antung on the Yalu.

The hills bordering the Yalu-Aiho Valley on the right bank—*i.e.*, on the N.-W. side—are not entirely unlike those about Telissu, but they do not attain such a maximum elevation.

Their surface soil is also softer, easily trenched, very red and conspicuous, and inclined to be shingly in places. Some of the narrower hilltops and ridges are rather rocky and rough. There is more cultivation about this country than in similar hilly tracts already described, and fields exist quite high up the hillsides. These hills are also more wooded, with patches of fir and other trees of an oak-like kind on their sides and in their valleys, and the grass is longer.

"Nullahs" are not quite so numerous or deeply-cut as in the country hitherto described, and hill-slopes are more rolling and "connected" in character. It is the kind of country that might be described as rather better suited to the movements of field artillery.

The hills on the right bank rise fairly steeply from the vicinity of the Yalu and Aiho to an average height of 400 to 500 feet, and a maximum (exclusive of the Phœnix Spur) of 1,100 feet. Lateral communication is not easy in these hills, and may only be had, directly, along the narrow level strip bordering the rivers.

The hilly country about Hu-Shan, in the angle enclosed by the Yalu and Aiho, appears to be rougher and steeper, and is of greater

DESCRIPTION OF MANCHURIA

general elevation. The TIGER HILL, at the junction of the YALU and AIHO, is isolated from the main range, and is a very rocky, bare, and steep little hill, rising abruptly to about 300 feet above the river.

The YALU-AIHO river-beds form a level stretch of sand, shingle, and water-channels, about three miles wide, divided up by the larger alluvial islands, such as CHOKODAI, OSEKI, and KINTEI. These islands are not quite flat, but undulate gently. Some considerable undulations, obviously old silted-up channels, traverse CHOKODAI ISLAND lengthwise, affording a considerable amount of cover.

The rich, deep soil of CHOKODAI is cultivated, and, besides the village of the same name, there are minor "steadings," or clusters of huts, on this island. A few small trees exist near these dwellings. In May the cultivated ground is bare and under plough.

The larger islands are quite open, but most of OSEKITO and the E. portion of KINTEITO and the neighbouring left bank of the river are rather thickly covered with osier-like bush and scrub. They are also somewhat sandy and shingly.

The main stream of the YALU averages about 400 yards wide, 6 feet deep, and runs at about three miles *per* hour over a shingly bottom. It is largely navigated by big sailing junks.

The AIHO channels average 200 yards wide, each branch, near their junction with the YALU, and are usually fordable. Current about two miles per hour, over a generally firm sandy bed.

The smaller streams, such as the HAMAT'UN RIVER, are typically Manchurian—shallow, with sandy beds.

The main impression gained on viewing the country about the YALU is surprise at the large extent of this battle-field, the whole terrain being much "bigger" than is perhaps gathered from a perusal of the map.

MAP A.

TO SHOW LOCATION OF SKETCHES A, B, C, D, E, AND F.

London: Hugh Rees, Ltd.

PORT ARTHUR. EASTERN DEFENCES, VIEWED FROM WESTERN CREST OF TAKUSHAN.

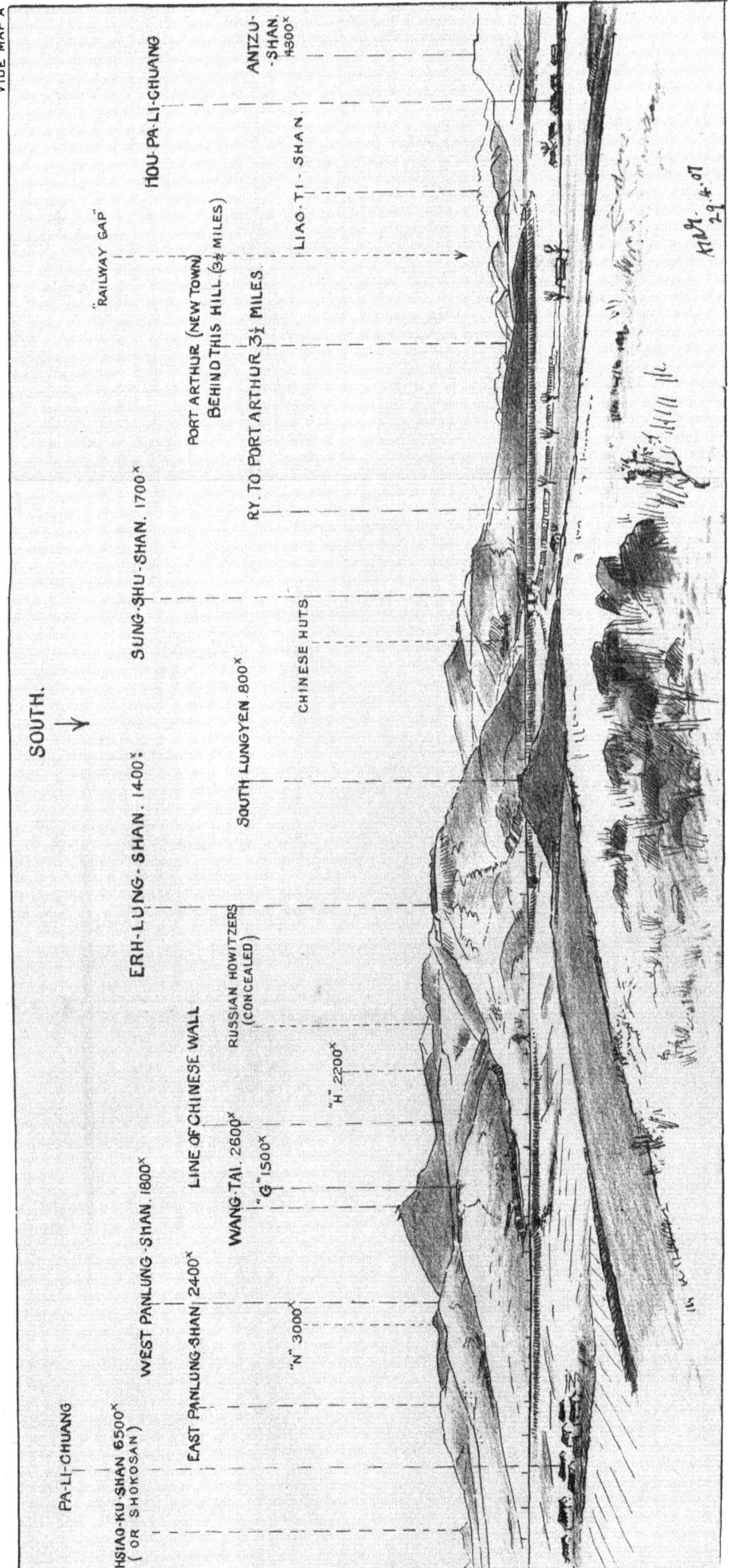

PORT ARTHUR. VIEW OF NORTHERN DEFENCES, FROM A POINT 150× SOUTH OF "Q", LOOKING SOUTHWARD.

SKETCH "C"
VIDE MAP "A"

ERHLUNGSHAN. 1400ˣ SUI-SHI-YING. 3900ˣ SOUTH LUNGYEN WORK 2100ˣ "H". 550 "Q". OR FORT KUROPATKIN. 3000ˣ PALICHUANG VILLAGE WEST PANLUNGSHAN 850ˣ

VIEW LOOKING N-W, FROM SUMMIT OF WANG-TAI. (BODAI.)

PORT ARTHUR. TWO COMPARATIVE VIEWS.

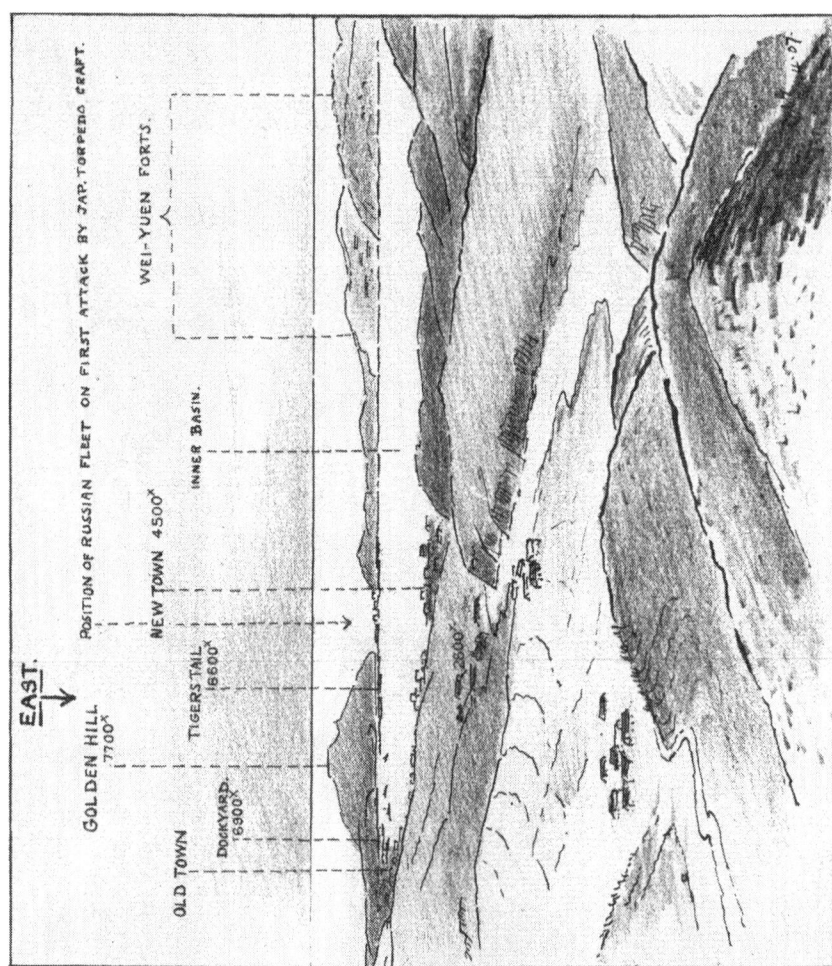

SKETCH "D.1."
VIDE MAP "A".

VIEW FROM TOP OF 203 METRE HILL, IN W. SECTOR OF RUSSIAN DEFENCES.

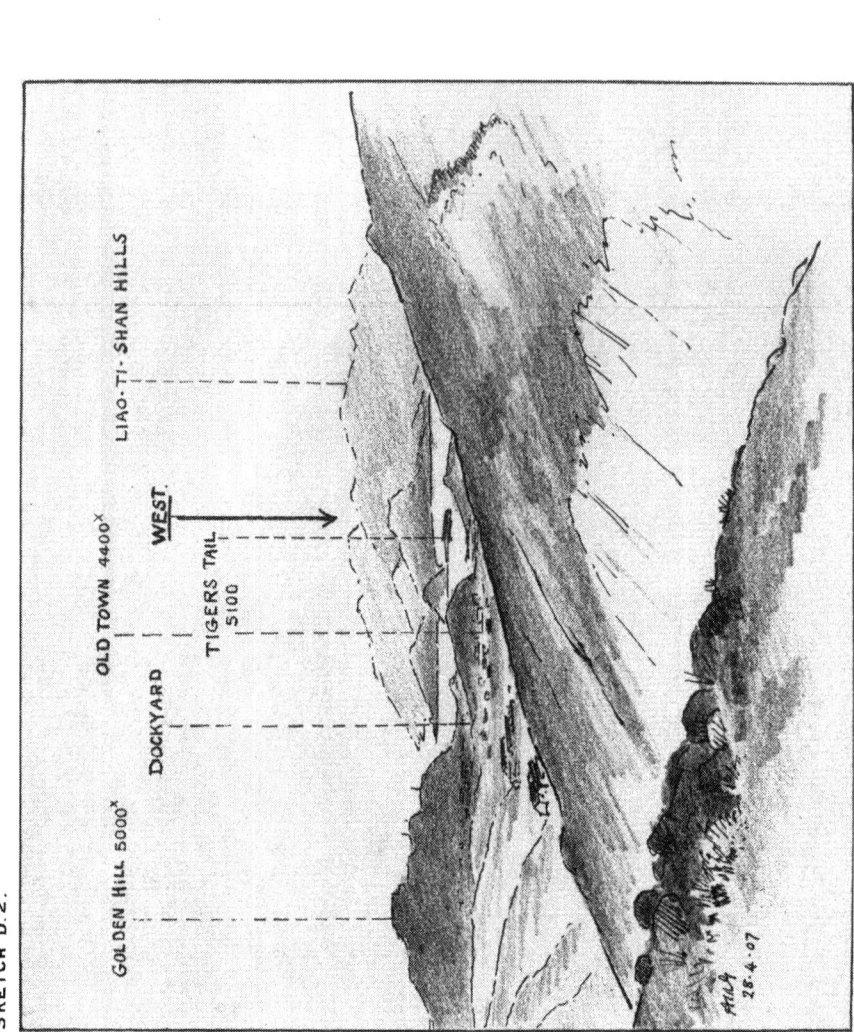

SKETCH "D.2".

VIEW FROM VICINITY OF EAST KIKWAN SHAN FORT, IN E. SECTOR OF RUSSIAN DEFENCES.

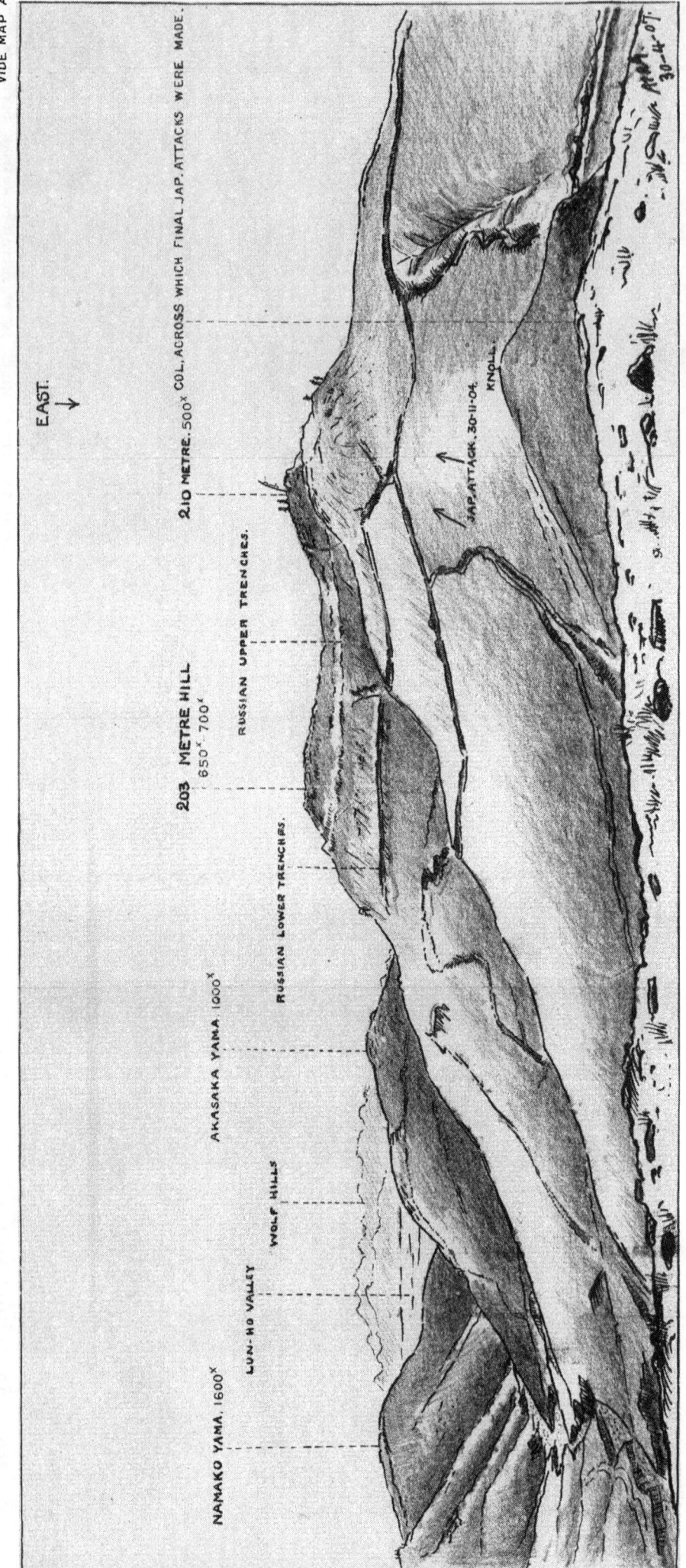

SKETCH E
VIDE MAP "A"

VIEW OF 203-METRE HILL, FROM "HILL 590", LOOKING EASTWARD.

SKETCH "F"
VIDE MAP "A"

AKASAKAYAMA. 500×

TRACK TO PORT ARTHUR

203-METRE HILL 500×

210-METRE

203-METRE HILL, FROM RAVINE BELOW N. SIDE

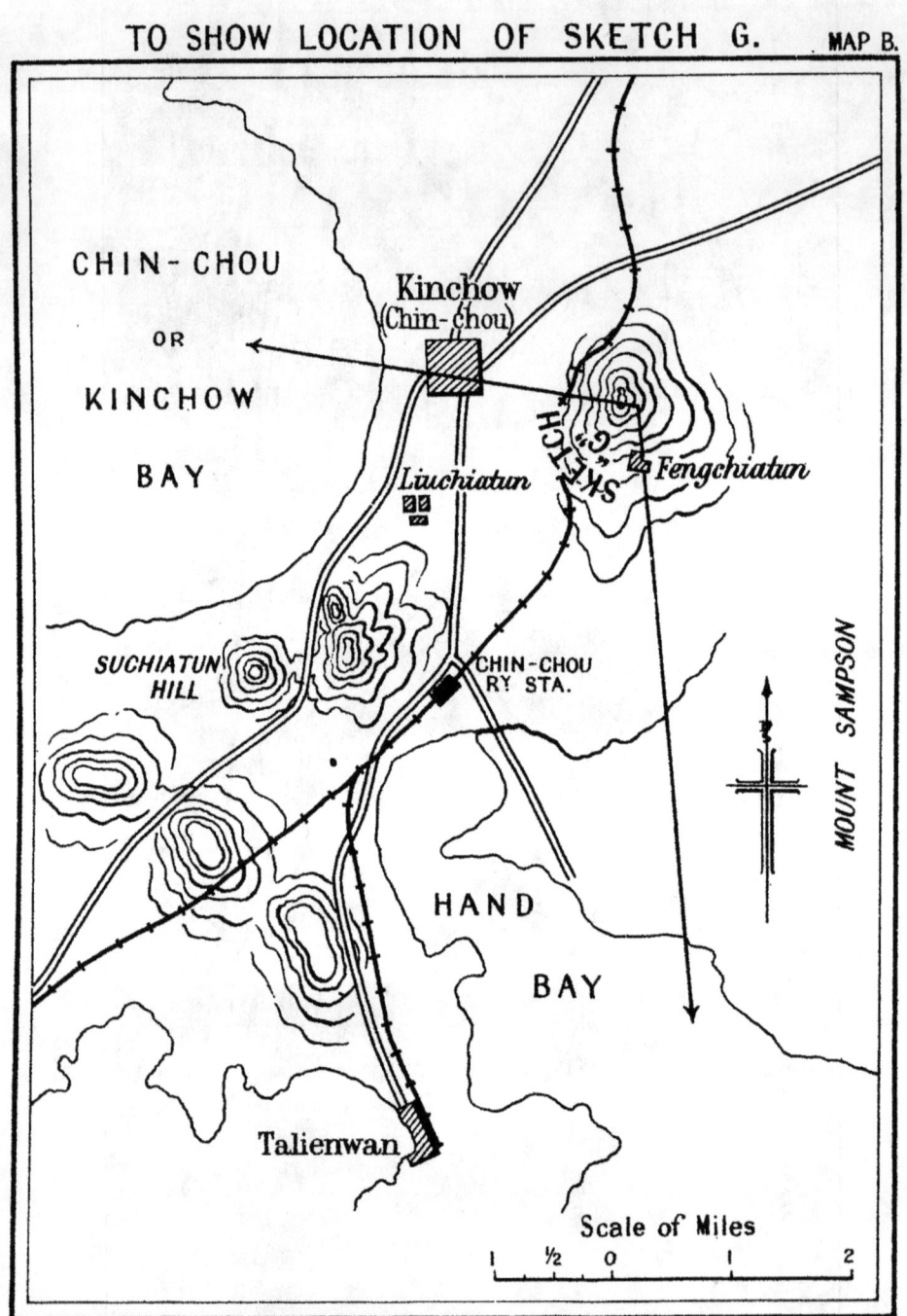

TO SHOW LOCATION OF SKETCH G.   MAP B.

NAN SHAN.

SKETCH "C"
VIDE MAP "B"

WEST →

FENG-CHIA-TUN (GEN¹ OKU'S H-Q)
DALNY.
HAND BAY.
CHIN-CHOU RY. STA.
RUSSIAN BARRACKS
HILLS NEAR PORT ARTHUR.
A B
NAN SHAN POSITION.
4500ˣ +350'
SSU-CHIA-TUN HILL 5500ˣ
C D
LIU-CHIA-TUN.
CHIN-CHOU BAY.
FORESHORE (LOW WATER)
CHIN-CHOU 2600ˣ

RY. TO MUKDEN →

VIEW OF THE RUSSIAN POSITION FROM THE JAPANESE H.Q.
"A" TO "B" WAS ATTACKED BY THE JAPANESE IIIrd DIVISION, "B" TO "C" BY THE I^st,
AND "C" TO "D" BY THE IVth.

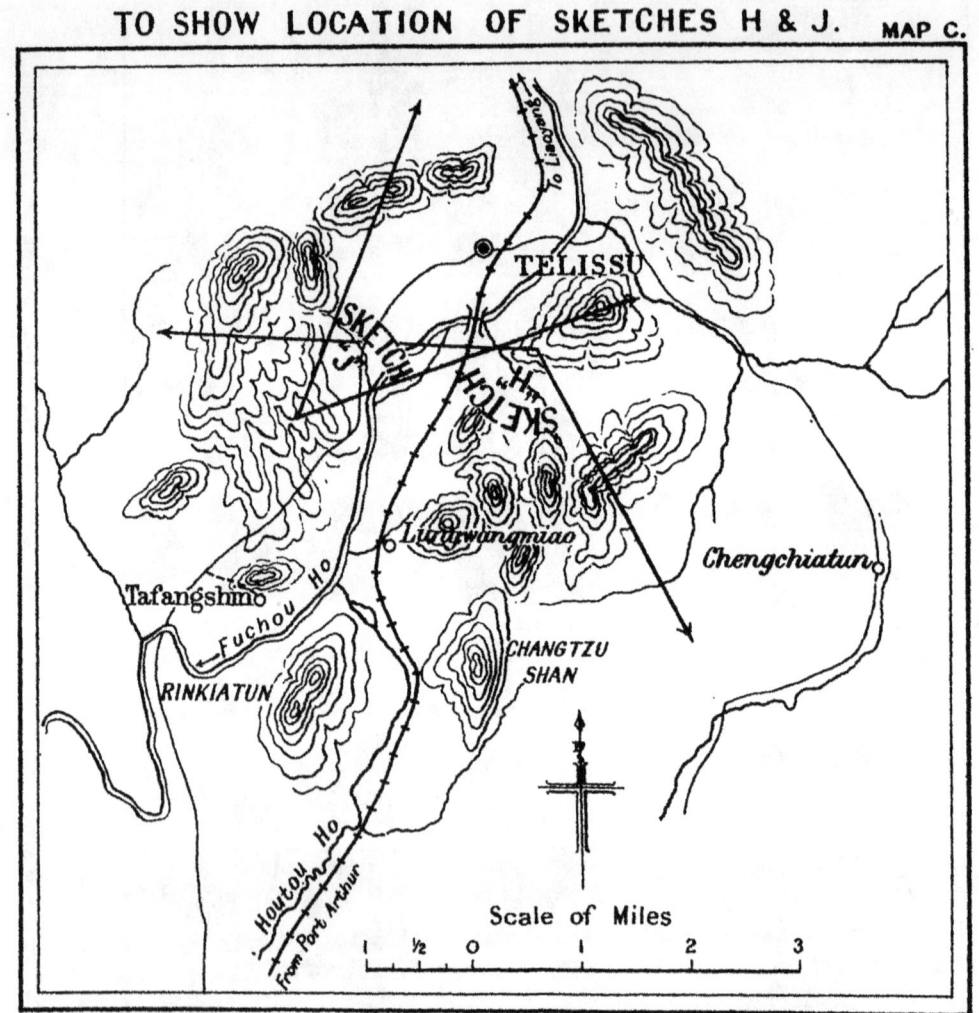

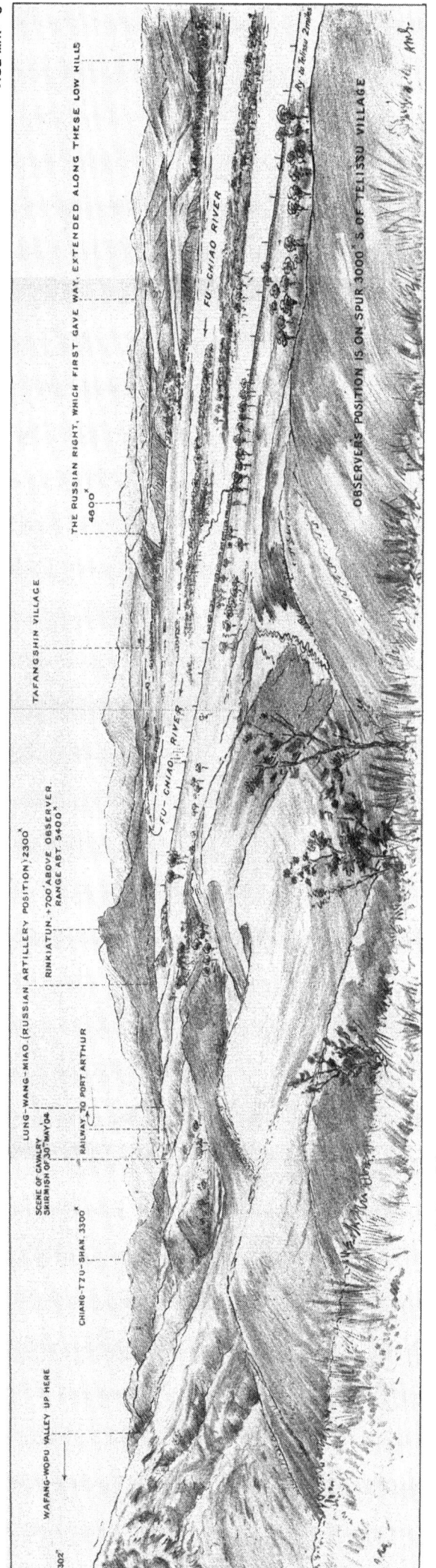

TELISSU. VIEW FROM BEHIND RUSSIAN CENTRE, LOOKING DOWN FU-CHIAO VALLEY.

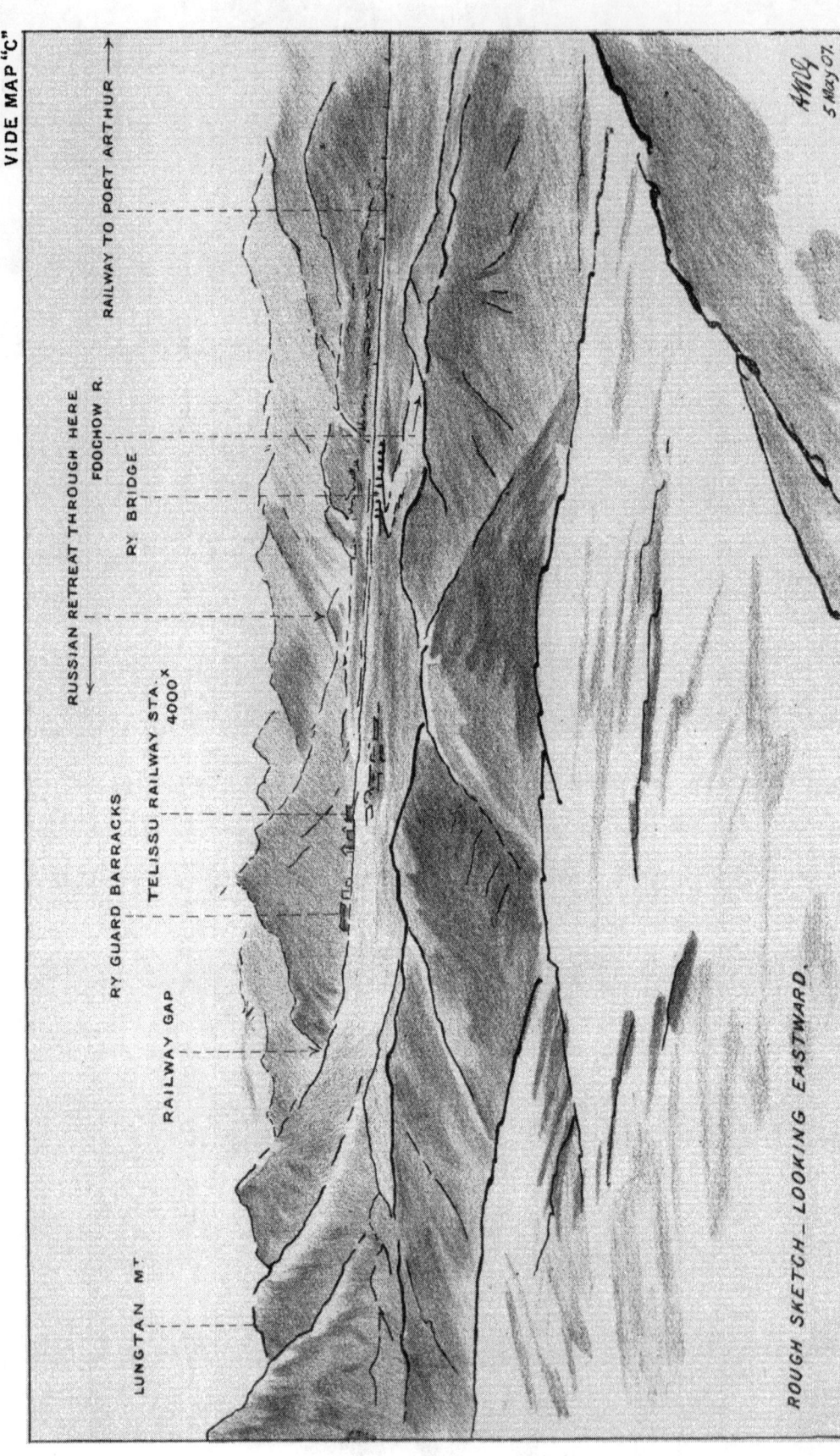

RIDGES ABANDONED BY RUSSIAN RIGHT AT TELISSU,

SHEWING HOW THE JAPANESE OVERLOOKED THE RUSSIAN RETIREMENT AND RAILWAY STATION.

TO SHOW LOCATION OF SKETCHES K, L, M, N, O, P, Q, & U.

MAP D.

SKETCH "K"
VIDE MAP "D"

SHOU-SHAN-PU. (BATTLE OF LIAOYANG.)

VIEW OF THE RUSSIAN POSITIONS FROM "HILL 224", 4 MILES S.W. OF SHOUSHANPU HILL.

ROUGH SKETCH OF THE RUSSIAN POSITIONS ON HILLS ABOUT 7 MILES S.E. OF LIAOYANG, AND NEAR TSAOFANT'UN.

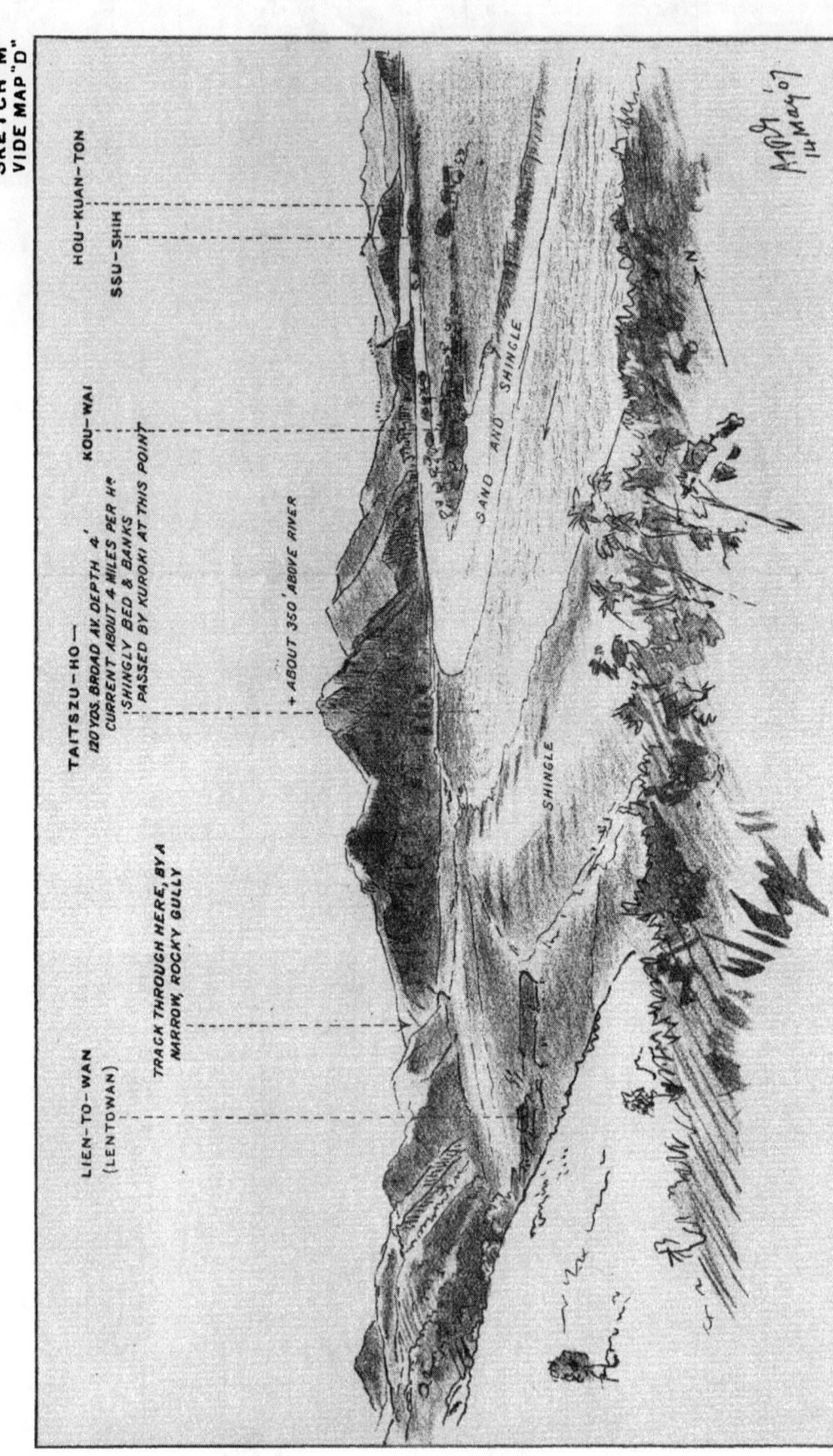

BATTLE OF LIAOYANG. KUROKI'S CROSSING OF THE TAITSE-HO AT LIENTOWAN.

SKETCH "N"
VIDE MAP "D"

HSI-KUAN-TUN HUAN-SHIN MANJUYAMA HEI-YEN-TAI

MANJUYAMA
RANGE ABOUT 5000ˣ
HEIGHT ABOVE PLAIN 150 TO 180 FT
(NOT 50' AS STATED BY SOME)

HILL 131

TAITSE-HO

14 May 07

MANJUYAMA, AS SEEN FROM BLUFF "A" 1 MILE N.W. OF YINGSHUPU VILLAGE.

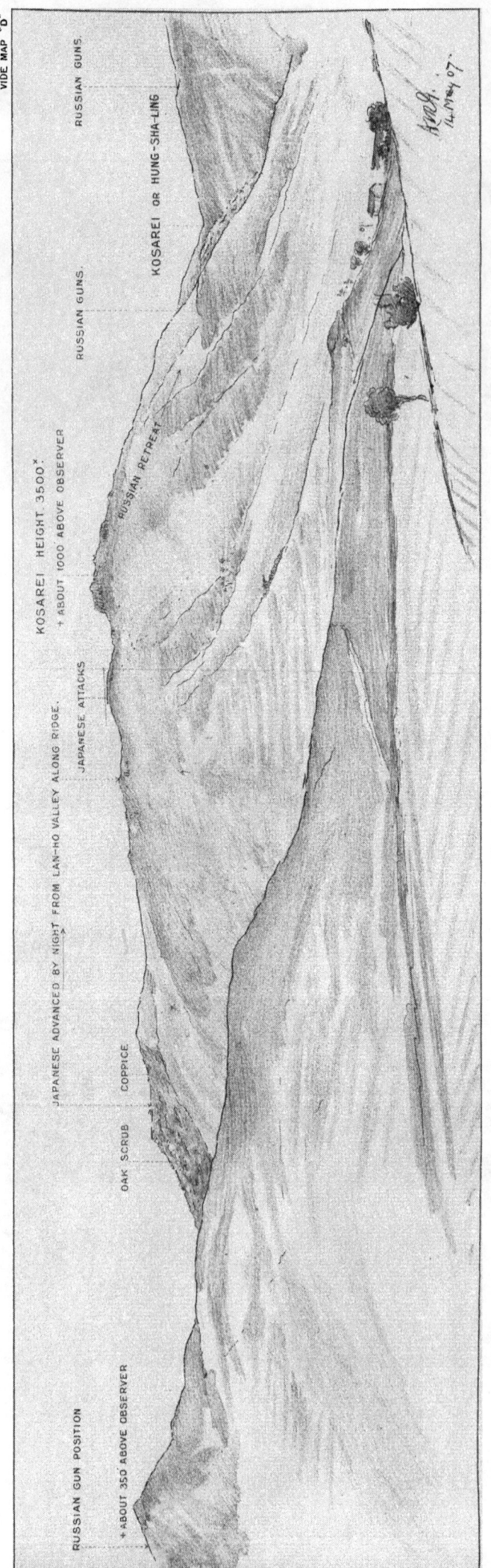

VIEW OF KOSAREI (OR HUNG-SHA-LING) HEIGHT, FROM PIAO-KAU VALLEY, LOOKING N.-E.

TYPICAL MOTIEN RANGE COUNTRY. VIEW FROM THE KUNG-CHANG-LING, LOOKING EASTWARD. ANPING IS BEHIND THE OBSERVER – 5 MILES OFF.

JAPANESE ADVANCED UP THIS VALLEY BY NIGHT, AND ATTACKED THE KUNG-CHANG LING AT DAWN.

SKETCH "P"
VIDE MAP "D"

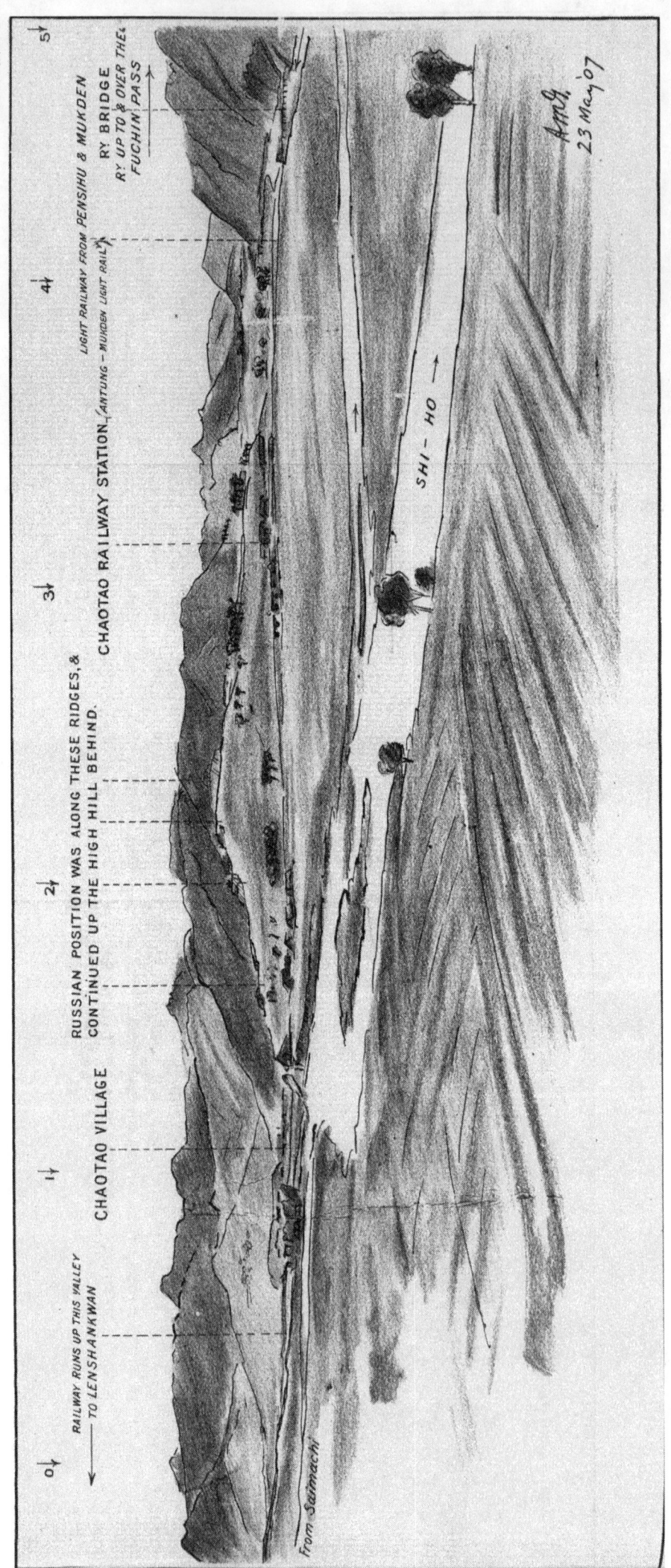

CHAOTAO.—ROUGH SKETCH OF THE RUSSIAN POSITION AT CHAO-TAO, LOOKING N.W. FROM LOWER SLOPE OF THE PRECIPITOUS BLUFFS ON RIGHT BANK OF THE SHI-HO

TO SHOW LOCATION OF SKETCHES R, S, & T.

MAP E.

London: Hugh Rees, Ltd. Stanford's Geogl. Establ., London.

SKETCH "R"
VIDE MAP "E"

PUTILOFF HILL
RANGE ABT 1 MILE
& ABT 50' ABOVE SURROUNDING PLAIN

OBELISK

TO-SAN
ABT 5 MILES

SHAHO RIVER

INTERIOR OF "NOVGOROD HILL" DEFENCES

"PUTILOFF HILL", LOOKING E. FROM "NOVGOROD HILL"

SKETCH "S"
VIDE MAP "E"

SAN-KWAI-SEKI-SAN 5200ˣ KOKASHI RIVER LINE JAPANESE ATTACK TERAYAMA 3500ˣ NANZAN 5800ˣ ROUND-TOP-HILL OKASAKIYAMA 6500ˣ SANKAISHI SURIBACHIYAMA ZENSHOTATZUKA AND YANJIN 4000ˣ HILLS NEAR IDAYAMA 8 TO 9 MILES

+ ABOUT 500′ ABOVE OBSERVER

HANLASANSHI VILLAGE — ABOUT 800ˣ
(PAN-LIAO-SHAN-TZŬ)

BATTLE OF THE SHAHO VIEW LOOKING NORTHWARD FROM N.E. END OF ISHIYAMA (1½ MILES N. OF YENTAI)

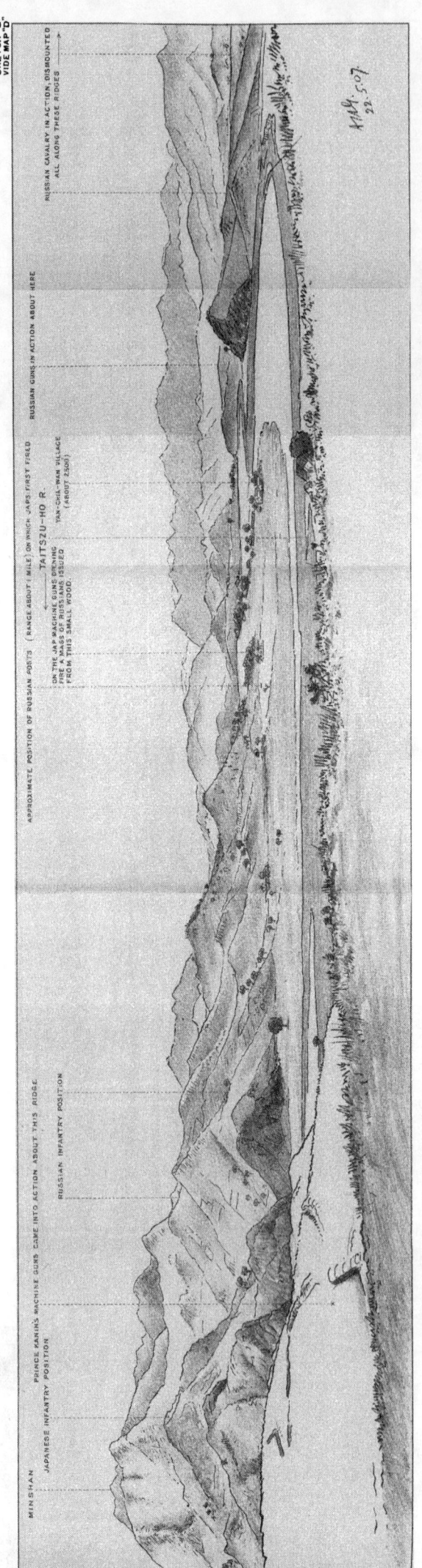

LOOKING UP THE TAITSE-HO VALLEY, ABOUT 3 MILES UPSTREAM FROM NEAR PENHSIHU. TO ILLUSTRATE PRINCE KANIN'S ACTION

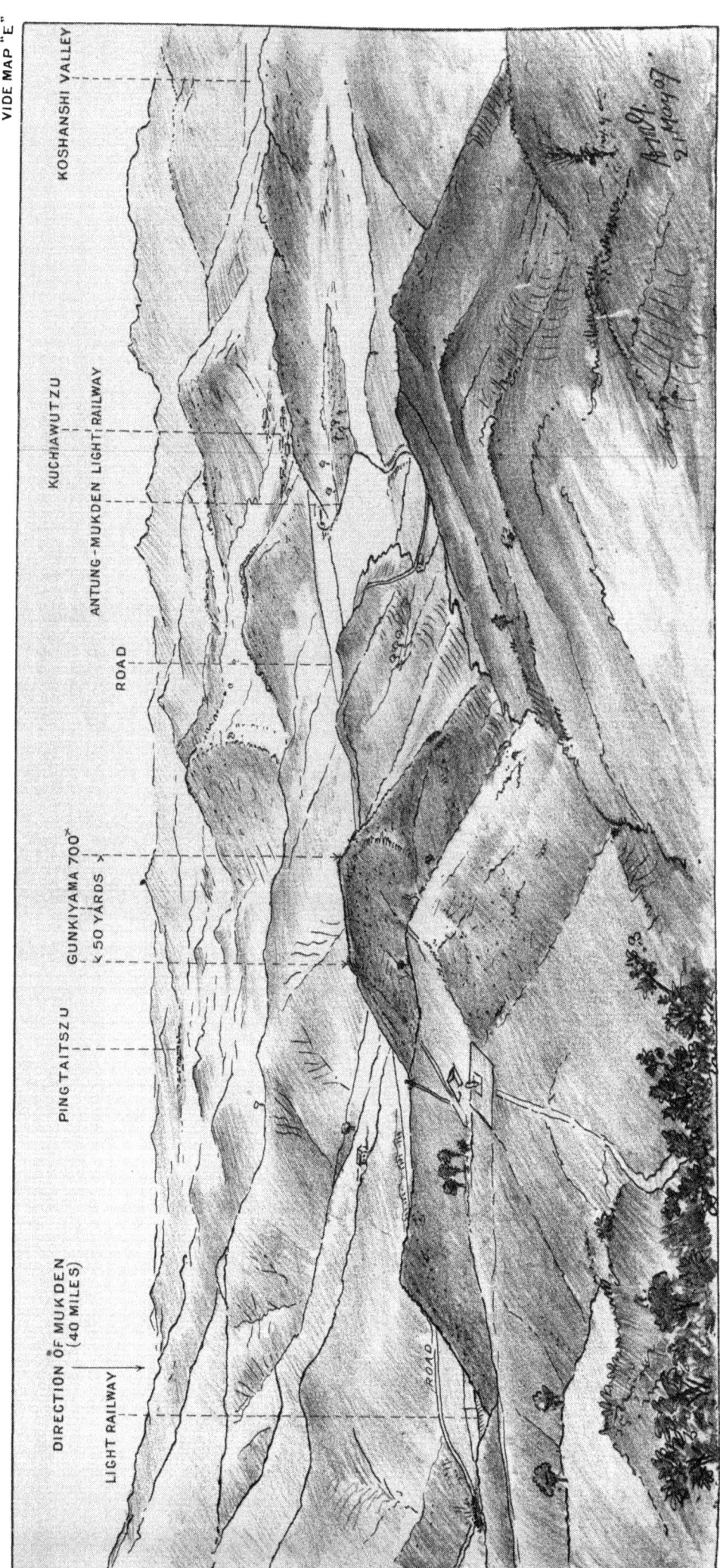

TA-LING.—VIEW LOOKING N., OVER GUNKIYAMA, FROM HIGH SPUR 600ˣ E. OF "PASS"

TO SHOW LOCATION OF SKETCHES V & W.

MAP F.

London: Hugh Rees, Ltd.

Stanford's Geogl. Establt, London

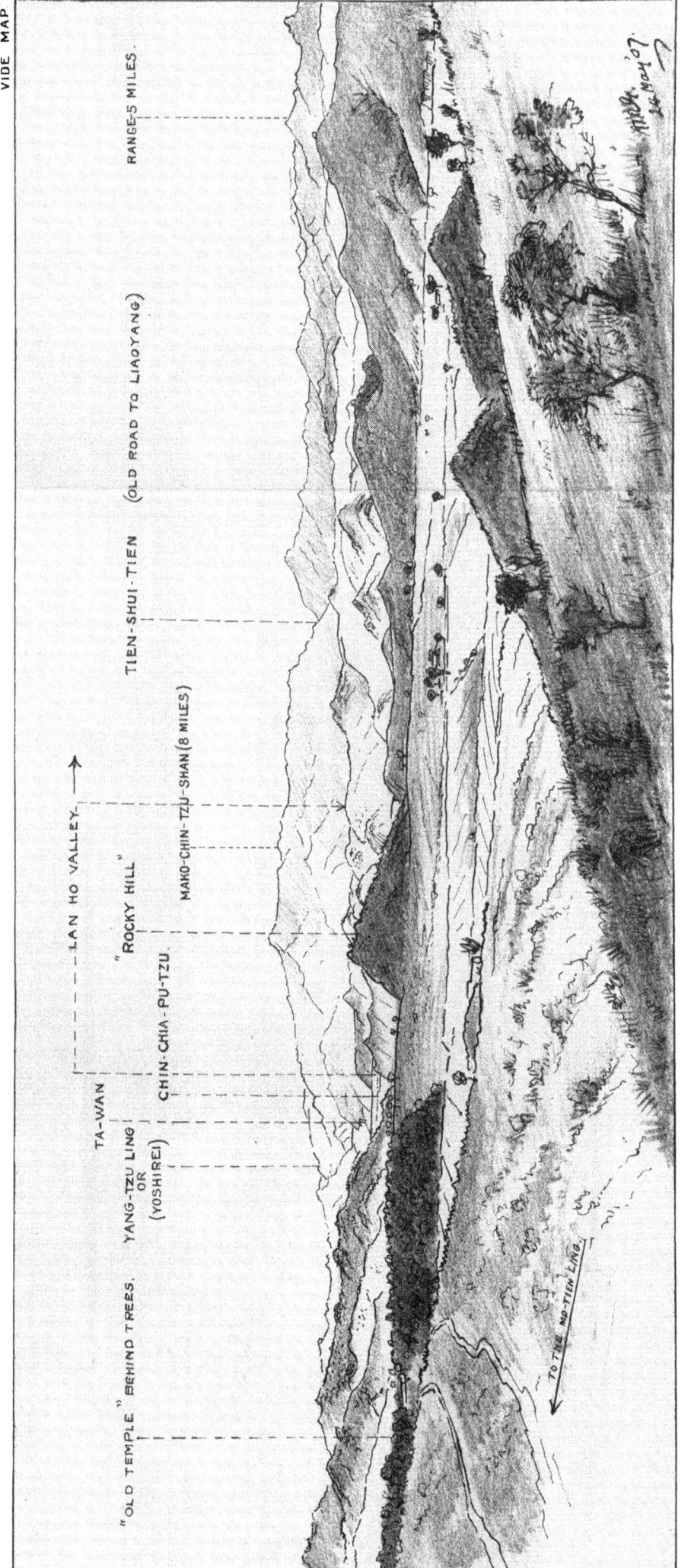

COUNTRY ROUND THE MO-TIEN LING. VIEW LOOKING WEST FROM NEW TEMPLE.

SKETCH "W"
VIDE MAP "F."

0 1 2 3 4

NEW TEMPLE | OLD TEMPLE BEHIND TREES | THICK WOODS OF OAK WITH UNDERGROWTH | RANGE ABOUT 1 MILE +200' ABOVE OBSERVER | RANGE ABOUT 1¾ MILES +ABOUT 700' ABOVE OBSERVER

ROAD

TO TAWAN →

"ROCKY HILL"

AMM 24.5.01

MOTIEN LING FROM WEST.

TO SHOW LOCATION OF SKETCHES X, Y, AND Z.

MAP G.

BATTLE OF THE YA-LU.

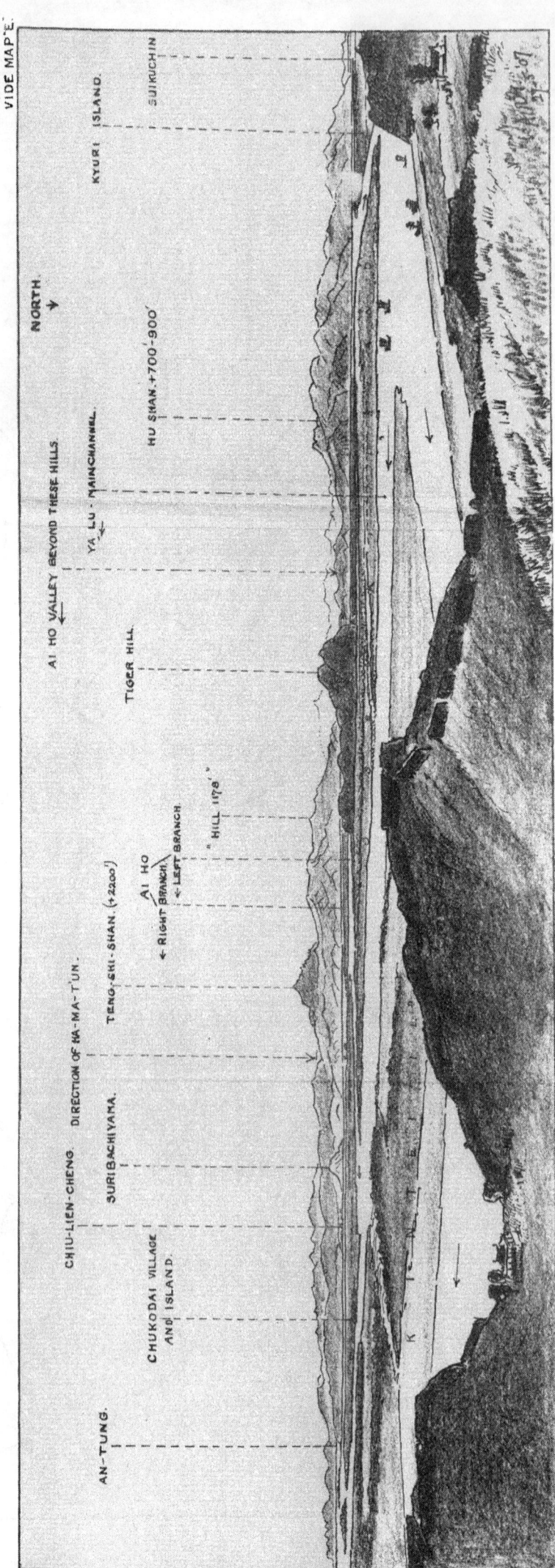

VIEW LOOKING ACROSS THE YA-LU & AI RIVERS TOWARDS THE RUSSIAN POSITIONS, FROM A TEMPLE NEAR WIJU, GENERAL KUROKI'S HD QRS DURING THE BATTLE.

SKETCH "Y"
VIDE MAP "G"

0 — JAP. 12TH DIVN. ADVANCED HERE
1
2 — SUI-KAU-CHIN BEYOND HERE
— HU-SHAN ± 700'–900'
— AI-HO LEFT BRANCH →
3 — TIGER HILL
— KYURI ISLAND
— OSEKI ISLAND
4 — YALU — MAIN CHANNEL
— TEMPLE NEAR WIJU-KUROKI'S H.Q.
— WIJU BEHIND RIDGE
5 — KINTEI ISLAND
— CHUKODAI VILLAGE
6

— ADVANCE OF JAP. GUARDS AND 2ND DIV.
— AI-HO RIGHT BRANCH
— CHUKODAI ISLAND

AnG
27 May 07

BATTLE OF THE YALU — VIEW OF JAPANESE SIDE FROM RUSSIAN POSITION. (AT SURIBACHIYAMA).

SKETCH "Z"
VIDE MAP "C"

JAP. 12TH DIVN CAME UP VALLEY BEHIND THIS HILL

LINE OF RETREAT OF RUSS.
R-G. FALLING BACK

KUEN-SHAN-TZU +570'

COTTAGES REACHED BY N° 5 COY
24TH JAPANESE REGT.

TENG-SHI-SHAN +2200'

HAMATUN IN HERE
POSITION OF CAPTURED
RUSSIAN GUNS

REARGUARD SURRENDERED
BEHIND RIDGE

TEN-SHUN-SHI

FINAL POSITION OF RUSSIAN REARGUARD

HAMATUN — VIEW LOOKING UP VALLEY FROM A POINT ABOUT 2 MILES W.S.W. OF CHIU-LIEN-CHENG.

www.ingramcontent.com/pod-product-compliance
Lightning Source LLC
Chambersburg PA
CBHW081544090426
42743CB00014BA/3133